COOK LIKE A PRO

Secrets and Must-Have Recipes

Table of Contents

INTRODUCTION

Welcome to **"Cook Like a Pro: Secrets and Must-Have Recipes"** This book is your guide to mastering the art of cooking like a pro, whether you're a seasoned chef or a beginner.

Discover essential techniques, mouthwatering recipes, and culinary inspiration that will elevate your cooking skills. From mastering the basics to exploring diverse dishes from around the world, this book will take you on a culinary journey like no other.

Get ready to impress your loved ones, expand your cooking repertoire, and savor the joy of creating delicious food. Let's embark on this exciting culinary adventure together!

Are you ready to cook like a pro? Let's dive in!

PART I

Essential Recipes for Every Home Chef

The Heart of Italian Cuisine

Homemade Pasta from Scratch

Classic Risotto Variations

Tantalizing Tiramisu

1. Homemade Pasta from Scratch

Homemade Pasta from Scratch

Introduction to the Dish:

Homemade Pasta from Scratch is a delightful culinary adventure that will elevate your appreciation for the simple yet extraordinary world of fresh pasta. This classic Italian dish is a testament to the magic that can be achieved with just a few basic ingredients and a touch of craftsmanship.

Ingredients:

- 2 cups of all-purpose flour
- 2 large eggs
- A pinch of salt
- *Optional*: 1 tablespoon of olive oil (for added richness)
- *Optional*: 1-2 tablespoons of water (if needed for the dough)
- *Optional Spices*: Freshly ground black pepper, a pinch of nutmeg, or finely chopped fresh herbs (e.g., basil, thyme, or parsley)

Step-by-Step Instructions:

Prepare the Work Surface: Start by clearing a clean, spacious work surface. Sprinkle a small amount of flour on the surface to prevent the pasta dough from sticking.

Create a Mound of Flour: On the floured surface, create a mound with the 2 cups of all-purpose flour. Make a well in the center of the mound, creating a crater-like shape.

Add Eggs and Salt: Crack the 2 large eggs into the well. Add a pinch of salt to the eggs. If desired, add 1 tablespoon of olive oil for added richness. You can also season with freshly ground black pepper, a pinch of nutmeg, or finely chopped fresh herbs if you'd like to enhance the flavor.

Begin Mixing: Using a fork, gently beat the eggs and optional olive oil, gradually incorporating the flour from the inner walls of the well. Continue mixing until a shaggy dough forms. If the dough is too dry, you can add 1-2 tablespoons of water as needed.

Knead the Dough: With your hands, start kneading the dough. Fold it in half, press it down, and rotate it a quarter turn. Repeat this process for about 8-10 minutes until the dough becomes smooth and elastic. If it's too dry, add a few drops of water; if too sticky, add a sprinkle of flour.

Rest the Dough: Wrap the pasta dough in plastic wrap and let it rest for at least 30 minutes at room temperature. This allows the gluten to relax and makes it easier to roll out.

Roll and Shape: Roll out the pasta dough using a pasta machine or a rolling pin until it reaches your desired thickness. You can now cut it into your preferred pasta shape, such as fettuccine, linguine, or tagliatelle.

Cook and Serve: Bring a large pot of salted water to a boil and cook the fresh pasta for about 2-4 minutes or until it floats to the surface. Drain and serve with your favorite sauce or toppings.

Tips:

- Fresh eggs and good-quality flour are key to excellent pasta.

- Don't skip the resting phase; it allows the dough to relax and prevents toughness.

- Experiment with different pasta shapes and sizes to create a variety of dishes.

- Fresh pasta pairs wonderfully with sauces like classic marinara, carbonara, or a simple garlic and olive oil dressing. You can also top it with grated Parmesan or Pecorino cheese for added flavor.

Enjoy your Homemade Pasta from Scratch with your choice of spices, sauces, and toppings as a delightful and satisfying culinary experience!

Classic Risotto Variations

Classic Risotto Variations take the rich, creamy, and comforting Italian rice dish to new heights. Whether you choose the classic preparation or experiment with optional ingredients, risotto is a versatile canvas for your culinary creativity.

Ingredients:

For Basic Risotto:

- 1+1/2 cups Arborio rice
- 4 cups chicken or vegetable broth (warmed)
- 1 cup dry white wine
- 1/2 cup finely chopped onion
- 2 tablespoons olive oil
- 2 cloves garlic (minced)
- 1/2 cup grated Parmesan cheese
- Salt and freshly ground black pepper to taste

Optional Ingredients:

- A splash of heavy cream for added creaminess
- 1/2 cup mushrooms (sliced) for a mushroom risotto
- 1/2 cup cooked and diced butternut squash for a squash risotto

Step-by-Step Instructions:

Sauté the Base: In a large skillet or saucepan, heat the olive oil over medium heat. Add the finely chopped onion and garlic. Sauté until the onion becomes translucent, about 2-3 minutes.

Toast the Rice: Add the Arborio rice to the pan and stir continuously for about 2 minutes. This toasting process enhances the nutty flavor of the rice.

Deglaze with Wine: Pour in the dry white wine and stir until it's mostly absorbed by the rice.

Add Broth Gradually: Begin adding the warm chicken or vegetable broth, one ladleful at a time, stirring frequently. Wait until each ladleful is mostly absorbed before adding more. Continue this process until the rice is creamy and cooked to your desired level of tenderness. This should take about 18-20 minutes.

Incorporate Optional Ingredients: If you're making a variation (e.g., mushroom, squash, or seafood risotto), add the optional ingredients when the rice is almost cooked through. This allows them to cook and meld with the risotto.

Finish with Cheese: Remove the risotto from heat, and stir in the grated Parmesan cheese. Season with salt and freshly ground black pepper to taste. For added creaminess, you can also add a splash of heavy cream at this stage.

- 1/2 cup cooked and diced shrimp for a seafood risotto
- Fresh herbs like thyme or sage for extra flavor

Suggested Pairings:

- A glass of white wine, such as Chardonnay or Pinot Grigio
- Crusty bread or a side salad with balsamic vinaigrette

Serve Hot: Risotto is best served immediately while it's creamy and piping hot. Garnish with fresh herbs if desired.

Tips:

- Use Arborio rice for the creamiest texture.

- Warm the broth before adding it to the rice to maintain a consistent temperature.

- Stirring is essential for a creamy risotto, but avoid over-stirring, which can make it gummy.

- Experiment with different optional ingredients and herbs to create unique risotto variations.

- Pair your risotto with a glass of white wine and a side of crusty bread or salad for a delightful meal.

Enjoy your Classic Risotto Variations as a comforting and versatile Italian dish!

3. Tantalizing Tiramisu

Tantalizing Tiramisu

Introduction to the Dish:

Tantalizing Tiramisu is a classic Italian dessert that embodies the essence of elegance and indulgence. This luscious dessert features layers of espresso-soaked ladyfingers and a rich mascarpone cream, all topped with a dusting of cocoa powder. It's a heavenly treat that's sure to captivate your taste buds.

Ingredients:

For the Tiramisu:

- 6 large egg yolks
- 3/4 cup granulated sugar
- 1 cup mascarpone cheese
- 1 1/2 cups heavy cream
- 2 cups brewed espresso or strong coffee, cooled
- 1/4 cup coffee liqueur (optional)
- 1 package of ladyfingers (approximately 24-30 ladyfingers)
- Unsweetened cocoa powder, for dusting
- Dark chocolate shavings or cocoa nibs (optional, for garnish)

Optional Ingredients:

- 1/4 cup coffee liqueur for a stronger coffee flavor
- Dark chocolate shavings or chocolate curls for extra elegance

Step-by-Step Instructions:

Prepare the Espresso: Brew the espresso or strong coffee and let it cool to room temperature. If desired, add coffee liqueur to the coffee for an extra kick.

Make the Mascarpone Cream: In a heatproof bowl, whisk together the egg yolks and granulated sugar until thick and pale. Place the bowl over a pot of simmering water (double boiler) and continue whisking for about 5 minutes until the mixture thickens. Remove from heat and let it cool.

Incorporate Mascarpone: Gently fold the mascarpone cheese into the cooled egg yolk mixture until well combined.

Whip the Cream: In a separate bowl, whip the heavy cream until stiff peaks form. Carefully fold the whipped cream into the mascarpone mixture until smooth and airy. This is your luscious mascarpone cream.

Dip and Layer Ladyfingers: Quickly dip each ladyfinger into the brewed espresso or coffee mixture (and coffee liqueur if used) for a few seconds until soaked but not soggy. Arrange a layer of dipped ladyfingers in the bottom of your serving dish.

Layer the Cream: Spread a portion of the mascarpone cream over the layer of ladyfingers.

Repeat and Chill: Repeat the layers until you run out of ingredients, typically ending with a layer of mascarpone cream on top. Cover and refrigerate for at least 4 hours, or ideally overnight, to allow the flavors to meld.

- A glass of Italian dessert wine, such as Vin Santo
- Fresh berries or a fruit compote for a fruity twist

Dust with Cocoa: Before serving, dust the top of the tiramisu generously with unsweetened cocoa powder. Optionally, garnish with dark chocolate shavings or curls.

Tips:

- Use fresh and high-quality ingredients for the best flavor.

- Adjust the sweetness to your preference by adding more or less sugar to the mascarpone cream.

- Allow the tiramisu to chill for several hours or overnight; this enhances the flavors and texture.

- Customize your tiramisu with coffee liqueur or additional espresso for a stronger coffee flavor.

- For an elegant presentation, consider adding dark chocolate shavings or curls as a garnish.

Enjoy your Tantalizing Tiramisu as a captivating and delectable Italian dessert!

Asian Culinary Adventures

Sushi and Sashimi Mastery

Thai Curry Creations

Chinese Dumpling Delights

4. Sushi and Sashimi Mastery

Sushi and Sashimi Mastery

Introduction to the Dish:

Sushi and Sashimi Mastery is the art of crafting exquisite Japanese cuisine that tantalizes the senses. Sushi showcases perfectly seasoned rice paired with fresh fish and other delectable ingredients, while sashimi highlights the pure essence of pristine seafood. This culinary journey is a testament to precision, balance, and the pursuit of culinary perfection.

Ingredients:

For Sushi and Sashimi:

- Sushi-grade fish (e.g., tuna, salmon, yellowtail)
- Sushi rice (short-grain Japanese rice)
- Nori (seaweed sheets)
- Wasabi paste
- Soy sauce (shoyu)
- Pickled ginger (gari)

Optional Ingredients:

- Avocado
- Cucumber
- Crab sticks
- Shrimp
- Scallions
- Sesame seeds
- Sriracha sauce
- Eel sauce (unagi sauce)

Suggested Pairings:

- A glass of sake or green tea

Step-by-Step Instructions:

For Sushi:

Prepare the Rice: Cook sushi rice following the package instructions, then season it with rice vinegar, sugar, and salt while it's still warm. Allow it to cool to room temperature.

Slice the Fish: Using a sharp knife, slice the sushi-grade fish into thin, uniform pieces. Cut against the grain for optimal texture.

Assemble Sushi Rolls: Lay a sheet of nori on a bamboo sushi mat covered with plastic wrap. Spread a thin layer of sushi rice evenly over the nori, leaving a small border. Add your choice of ingredients (fish, vegetables, or avocado), and roll it tightly using the bamboo mat.

Slice the Rolls: Wet your knife to prevent sticking, and slice the sushi rolls into bite-sized pieces. Clean the knife between cuts.

Serve with Condiments: Serve your sushi rolls with wasabi, soy sauce, and pickled ginger.

For Sashimi:

Select the Freshest Fish: Choose sushi-grade fish that is exceptionally fresh, free from any off-putting odors, and properly handled.

- Miso soup or seaweed salad as appetizers

Slice with Precision: Use a sharp, non-serrated knife to slice the fish thinly and diagonally. Present the slices on a chilled platter.

Garnish Simply: Arrange the sashimi slices with minimal garnish to highlight the purity of the fish. Suggested garnishes include thinly sliced cucumbers or daikon radish.

Tips:

- Purchase sushi-grade fish from a reputable seafood market or supplier.

- Keep your hands moistened when working with sushi rice to prevent sticking.

- Experiment with different ingredients to create unique sushi rolls.

- Practice precision and patience in slicing to achieve beautiful and delicate sashimi pieces.

- Serve sushi and sashimi with wasabi, soy sauce, and pickled ginger for an authentic experience.

Enjoy your journey to Sushi and Sashimi Mastery as you craft these exquisite Japanese dishes!

5. Thai Curry Creations

Thai Curry Creations

<u>**Introduction to the Dish:**</u>

Thai Curry Creations invite you to embark on a culinary journey through the vibrant and aromatic world of Thai cuisine. With a fragrant Thai curry base and a variety of protein and vegetable options, you can create a masterpiece that's tailored to your taste buds.

<u>**Ingredients:**</u>

For Thai Curry Base:

- 2 tablespoons Thai red curry paste (adjust for spice level)
- 1 can (14 ounces) coconut milk
- 1-2 tablespoons vegetable oil
- 1 tablespoon fish sauce (or soy sauce for a vegetarian version)
- 1 tablespoon palm sugar (or brown sugar)
- 1-2 kaffir lime leaves (optional, for extra flavor)
- Thai basil leaves (for garnish)

Protein Options:

- 1 pound boneless chicken, beef, shrimp, tofu, or vegetables

<u>**Step-by-Step Instructions:**</u>

Prepare the Thai Curry Base:

Heat the vegetable oil in a wok or large skillet over medium-high heat.
Add the minced garlic, galangal or ginger, and lemongrass. Sauté for a minute until fragrant.

Add the Curry Paste:

Stir in the Thai red curry paste and cook for 1-2 minutes to release its flavors.

Incorporate the Protein:

Add the chosen protein (chicken, beef, shrimp, tofu, or vegetables) and cook until it's almost done.

Pour in Coconut Milk:

Pour in the coconut milk and stir to combine. Bring the mixture to a gentle simmer.

Season and Sweeten:

Add fish sauce (or soy sauce for a vegetarian version), palm sugar (or brown sugar), and kaffir lime leaves (if using). Adjust the seasonings to your taste.

Vegetable Options:

- Bell peppers, bamboo shoots, baby corn, snow peas, or eggplant

Aromatics:

- 2-3 cloves garlic (minced)
- 1-2 slices of galangal or ginger
- 1-2 stalks of lemongrass (smashed and cut into pieces)
- Thai bird's eye chili (for extra heat, optional)

Suggested Pairings:

- Steamed jasmine rice or rice noodles
- Thai cucumber salad or papaya salad as a side dish
- Thai iced tea or coconut water to complement the meal

Add Vegetables:

Add the chosen vegetables and simmer until they're tender but still crisp.

Simmer to Perfection:

Allow the curry to simmer for a few more minutes, letting the flavors meld together.

Garnish and Serve:

Remove the lemongrass pieces and kaffir lime leaves (if used). Garnish with Thai basil leaves.
Serve your Thai curry creations hot with steamed jasmine rice or rice noodles.

Tips:

- Adjust the level of spice by adding more or less Thai red curry paste or chili.

- Experiment with different proteins and vegetables to create a variety of Thai curry dishes.

- Use fresh, high-quality ingredients for the best flavor.

- Serve Thai cucumber salad or papaya salad as a refreshing side dish to complement the richness of the curry.

- Balance the flavors by adjusting the fish sauce (for saltiness), palm sugar (for sweetness), and lime juice (for acidity).

Enjoy your Thai Curry Creations as you savor the vibrant and aromatic flavors of Thai cuisine!

Chinese Dumpling Delights

Introduction to the Dish:

Chinese Dumpling Delights invite you to master the art of crafting these delectable parcels of flavor. Filled with a savory mixture of ground pork, vegetables, and seasonings, and wrapped in thin dumpling wrappers, these dumplings offer a delightful combination of taste and texture.

Ingredients:

For Dumpling Filling:

- 1 pound ground pork (or your choice of protein)
- 2 cups finely chopped napa cabbage
- 2 cloves garlic (minced)
- 1 tablespoon fresh ginger (minced)
- 2-3 green onions (finely chopped)
- 1 tablespoon soy sauce
- 1 tablespoon oyster sauce (optional)
- 1 teaspoon sesame oil
- Salt and pepper to taste

Dumpling Wrappers:

- Store-bought dumpling wrappers or homemade dumpling dough

Dipping Sauce:

- Soy sauce
- Rice vinegar

Step-by-Step Instructions:

Prepare the Dumpling Filling:

In a large bowl, combine the ground pork, chopped napa cabbage, minced garlic, minced ginger, chopped green onions, soy sauce, oyster sauce (if using), sesame oil, salt, and pepper. Mix well until everything is evenly combined.

Assemble the Dumplings:

- Take a dumpling wrapper and place a spoonful of the filling in the center (about 1 tablespoon). Be careful not to overfill.
- Moisten the edge of the wrapper with a little water to help with sealing.
- Fold the wrapper in half to create a half-moon shape, then press the edges together to seal. You can use pleating techniques for decorative edges if desired.

Cook the Dumplings:

You can prepare Chinese Dumpling Delights in various ways:
- **Boiling**: Boil dumplings in a pot of water until they float to the surface and cook for an additional 1-2 minutes.
- **Steaming**: Steam dumplings in a bamboo steamer or a steamer basket for about 15-20 minutes.

- Sesame oil
- Minced garlic
- Red chili flakes (optional)

Optional Ingredients for Filling:

- Shrimp, finely chopped mushrooms, tofu, or other favorite ingredients

Suggested Pairings:

- Hot and sour soup or egg drop soup as appetizers
- Steamed or stir-fried vegetables as a side dish
- Jasmine tea or Chinese green tea to accompany the meal

- **Pan-Frying**: Pan-fry dumplings in a lightly oiled skillet until the bottoms are golden brown, then add water to the pan, cover, and steam until fully cooked.

Make the Dipping Sauce:

In a small bowl, combine soy sauce, rice vinegar, sesame oil, minced garlic, and red chili flakes (if desired) to create a dipping sauce.

Serve and Enjoy:

Arrange the cooked dumplings on a platter and serve hot with the dipping sauce.

Tips:

- Customize the filling by adding your choice of protein (e.g., shrimp, mushrooms, tofu) or additional vegetables.

- Be mindful not to overfill the dumplings, as they may burst during cooking.

- Ensure a tight seal when folding dumplings to prevent them from opening while cooking.

- Experiment with different cooking methods for varied textures and flavors.

- Serve with a dipping sauce that suits your taste, adjusting the ingredients to achieve the desired balance of flavors.

Enjoy your Chinese Dumpling Delights as you savor the delicious taste and artistry of homemade dumplings!

Mouthwatering Main Courses

Honey-Glazed Pork Ribs

Crispy Fried Chicken

Steamed Lime Herb Fish

7. Honey-Glazed Pork Ribs

Honey-Glazed Pork Ribs

Introduction to the Dish:

Honey-Glazed Pork Ribs are a succulent and flavorful dish that embodies the perfect balance of sweetness, saltiness, and smokiness. These tender ribs, coated in a luscious honey glaze, are sure to tantalize your taste buds and make any meal special.

Ingredients:

For Honey-Glazed Pork Ribs:

- 2 racks of pork ribs (approximately 4-5 pounds)
- 1/2 cup honey
- 1/4 cup soy sauce
- 2 tablespoons Dijon mustard
- 2 tablespoons brown sugar
- 2 cloves garlic (minced)
- 1 teaspoon paprika
- 1/2 teaspoon black pepper
- 1/2 teaspoon salt
- Cooking oil for brushing

Optional Ingredients:

- A pinch of red pepper flakes for a spicy kick
- Freshly chopped cilantro or green onions for garnish

Suggested Pairings:

Step-by-Step Instructions:

Prepare the Ribs:

Remove the membrane from the back of the ribs (if not already removed) to ensure tenderness. Use a knife to gently lift the membrane from one end and peel it off.

Create the Marinade:

In a bowl, combine honey, soy sauce, Dijon mustard, brown sugar, minced garlic, paprika, black pepper, and salt. If you want a hint of heat, add a pinch of red pepper flakes.

Marinate the Ribs:

Place the pork ribs in a large resealable plastic bag or a shallow dish.
Pour the marinade over the ribs, making sure they are well coated. Seal the bag or cover the dish and refrigerate for at least 2 hours, or ideally overnight.

Preheat the Grill:

Preheat your grill to medium-high heat (about 350-375°F or 175-190°C). Set up for indirect grilling if possible.

Grill the Ribs:

Remove the ribs from the marinade and let excess marinade drip off.
Brush the grill grates with cooking oil to prevent sticking.

- Coleslaw or potato salad as side dishes
- Cornbread or garlic bread for a comforting meal
- Iced tea or a light lager beer to complement the flavors

Place the ribs on the grill, bone side down. Cover and grill for about 25-30 minutes, turning occasionally.

Apply the Honey Glaze:

During the last 10-15 minutes of cooking, start brushing the ribs with the honey glaze. Apply multiple layers, allowing each layer to caramelize before adding the next.

Check Doneness:

The ribs are done when the internal temperature reaches about 145°F (63°C) for pork ribs, and they are tender with a caramelized glaze.

Rest and Slice:

Remove the ribs from the grill and let them rest for a few minutes before slicing. This helps the juices redistribute and keeps the ribs moist.

Garnish and Serve:

Optionally, garnish the honey-glazed pork ribs with freshly chopped cilantro or green onions for a pop of color and flavor.

<u>**Tips:**</u>

- Adjust the sweetness and heat of the glaze to your preference by modifying the amount of honey and red pepper flakes.

- For extra tenderness, consider wrapping the ribs in aluminum foil and cooking them over indirect heat for a longer period.

- Don't rush the grilling process; slow and steady cooking yields the best results.

- Serve with classic barbecue sides like coleslaw or potato salad, and enjoy!

Savor your Honey-Glazed Pork Ribs as they deliver a mouthwatering blend of flavors and tender meat with a delightful glaze!

8. Crispy Fried Chicken

Crispy Fried Chicken

<u>**Introduction to the Dish:**</u>

Crispy Fried Chicken is a beloved comfort food that boasts golden, crunchy perfection on the outside and tender, flavorful meat on the inside. Whether you're enjoying it as a picnic treat or a Sunday dinner, this classic dish never fails to satisfy.

<u>**Ingredients:**</u>

For Crispy Fried Chicken:

- 4-6 chicken pieces (drumsticks, thighs, wings, or breast)
- 2 cups buttermilk (for marinating)
- 2 cups all-purpose flour
- 1 tablespoon paprika
- 1 teaspoon garlic powder
- 1 teaspoon onion powder
- 1 teaspoon salt
- 1/2 teaspoon black pepper
- 1/2 teaspoon cayenne pepper (adjust for spice level)
- Vegetable oil for frying

Optional Ingredients:

- Hot sauce or cayenne pepper for a spicy kick
- Fresh herbs like thyme or rosemary for added flavor

Suggested Pairings:

<u>**Step-by-Step Instructions:**</u>

Marinate the Chicken:

Place the chicken pieces in a bowl and pour the buttermilk over them. Ensure the chicken is well coated. Marinate in the refrigerator for at least 2 hours, or ideally overnight for maximum flavor.

Prepare the Coating:

In a shallow dish, combine the all-purpose flour, paprika, garlic powder, onion powder, salt, black pepper, and cayenne pepper. Mix thoroughly.

Coat the Chicken:

- Remove the chicken from the buttermilk and let the excess liquid drip off.
- Dredge each piece of chicken in the seasoned flour mixture, pressing the coating onto the chicken to ensure it adheres well. Shake off any excess flour.

Heat the Oil:

Fill a deep skillet or a Dutch oven with vegetable oil to a depth of about 2 inches. Heat the oil to 350-375°F (175-190°C) over medium-high heat.

Fry the Chicken:

- Mashed potatoes or coleslaw as side dishes
- Biscuits or cornbread for a classic Southern meal
- Sweet tea or lemonade to quench your thirst

- Carefully place the coated chicken pieces into the hot oil, a few at a time, depending on the size of your cooking vessel. Do not overcrowd the pan; this ensures even cooking.
- Fry the chicken for about 12-15 minutes per side (or until the internal temperature reaches 165°F or 74°C), turning occasionally to achieve even browning and crispy texture.

Drain and Rest:

- Use a slotted spoon or tongs to remove the fried chicken from the oil. Place the chicken on a wire rack or paper towels to drain excess oil.
- Allow the chicken to rest for a few minutes before serving; this helps maintain its juiciness.

Serve and Enjoy:

Serve your crispy fried chicken hot, with your choice of sides and dipping sauces.

<u>Tips:</u>

- Adjust the spice level to your liking by increasing or decreasing the amount of cayenne pepper.

- For an extra kick, brush the fried chicken with hot sauce immediately after frying.

- Maintain a consistent oil temperature for even cooking and a crispier texture.

- Use a meat thermometer to ensure the chicken reaches an internal temperature of 165°F (74°C) for safe consumption.

- Pair your crispy fried chicken with classic Southern sides and a refreshing beverage for the ultimate comfort meal.

Indulge in the crispy, flavorful goodness of homemade Crispy Fried Chicken for a memorable and satisfying dining experience!

Steamed Lime Herb Fish

Steamed Lime Herb Fish is a culinary masterpiece that celebrates the bright and zesty flavors of fresh herbs and citrus. This dish offers a delicate balance of fragrant herbs, tangy lime, and tender fish, making it a refreshing and healthy option for any meal.

Ingredients:

For Steamed Lime Herb Fish:

- 4 fish fillets (such as cod, tilapia, or sea bass), about 6-8 ounces each
- 2 limes (zest and juice)
- 2 cloves garlic (minced)
- 2 tablespoons fresh cilantro (chopped)
- 2 tablespoons fresh mint leaves (chopped)
- 2 tablespoons fresh basil leaves (chopped)
- 2 tablespoons fish sauce
- 1 tablespoon soy sauce (low-sodium)
- 1 tablespoon honey
- 1/2 teaspoon red pepper flakes (adjust for spice level)
- Salt and black pepper to taste

Step-by-Step Instructions:

Prepare the Fish:

Rinse the fish fillets and pat them dry with paper towels. Place them on a plate or a tray.

Create the Marinade:

In a bowl, combine the lime zest, lime juice, minced garlic, chopped cilantro, chopped mint leaves, chopped basil leaves, fish sauce, soy sauce, honey, red pepper flakes, salt, and black pepper. Mix well to create the marinade.

Marinate the Fish:

Pour the marinade over the fish fillets, ensuring they are well coated. Cover the fish and marinate in the refrigerator for about 20-30 minutes to infuse the flavors.

Prepare for Steaming:

Set up a steamer or a bamboo steamer over a pot of simmering water. Make sure the water doesn't touch the bottom of the steamer basket.

Steam the Fish:

Optional Ingredients:

- Sliced red chili for extra heat
- Sliced green onions for garnish
- Steamed jasmine rice or rice noodles for serving

Suggested Pairings:

- Steamed or stir-fried vegetables, such as broccoli or bok choy
- A light white wine or a crisp Sauvignon Blanc to complement the flavors

- Place the marinated fish fillets on a heatproof plate that fits inside your steamer basket.
- Cover the steamer with a lid and steam the fish for approximately 10-15 minutes, or until the fish flakes easily with a fork and is cooked through.

Serve:

- Carefully remove the plate with the steamed fish from the steamer.
- Garnish the fish with sliced red chili and sliced green onions (if desired).
- Serve your Steamed Lime Herb Fish hot, accompanied by steamed jasmine rice or rice noodles and your choice of vegetables.

Tips:

- Use fresh, high-quality fish for the best flavor and texture.

- Adjust the amount of red pepper flakes to control the level of spiciness.

- Be mindful of the steaming time to prevent overcooking; fish should be tender and moist.
- Serve the fish immediately to enjoy it at its best.

- Experiment with different herb combinations or citrus fruits for variety.

Savor the vibrant and aromatic flavors of Steamed Lime Herb Fish as you indulge in a healthy and delightful culinary experience!

Irresistible Desserts

Decadent Red Velvet Cake

Fresh Strawberry Cheesecake

Homemade Chocolate Truffles

Decadent Red Velvet Cake

Introduction to the Dish:

Decadent Red Velvet Cake is a beloved dessert that combines the rich flavor of chocolate with a hint of tanginess, creating a luxurious and visually stunning treat. Its striking red color and velvety texture make it the perfect choice for special occasions and celebrations.

Ingredients:

For the Red Velvet Cake:

- 2+1/2 cups all-purpose flour
- 1+1/2 cups granulated sugar
- 1+1/2 cups vegetable oil
- 1 cup buttermilk
- 2 large eggs
- 2 tablespoons unsweetened cocoa powder
- 1 teaspoon baking soda
- 1 teaspoon white vinegar
- 1 teaspoon vanilla extract
- 1 tablespoon red food coloring (adjust for desired color)
- 1/2 teaspoon salt

For Cream Cheese Frosting:

Step-by-Step Instructions:

For the Red Velvet Cake:

Preheat the Oven:

Preheat your oven to 350°F (175°C). Grease and flour two 9-inch round cake pans.

Mix Dry Ingredients:

In a bowl, combine the all-purpose flour, cocoa powder, and salt. Set aside.

Prepare the Buttermilk Mixture:

In a separate bowl, mix the buttermilk and red food coloring until well combined. Set aside.

Cream Sugar and Oil:

In a large mixing bowl, beat together the granulated sugar and vegetable oil until well combined and slightly fluffy.

Add Eggs and Vanilla:

Add the eggs one at a time, mixing well after each addition. Stir in the vanilla extract.

- 8 ounces cream cheese (softened)
- 1/2 cup unsalted butter (softened)
- 4 cups powdered sugar
- 1 teaspoon vanilla extract
- Optional Ingredients:

- Chopped pecans or walnuts for cake decoration
- Fresh raspberries or strawberries for garnish

Suggested Pairings:

- A tall glass of cold milk or a cup of coffee to complement the cake's sweetness
- Vanilla bean ice cream for an indulgent treat

Alternate Wet and Dry Ingredients:

Gradually add the dry flour mixture and the buttermilk mixture to the sugar and oil mixture, beginning and ending with the dry ingredients. Mix until just combined.

Add Vinegar and Baking Soda:

In a small bowl, combine the baking soda and white vinegar. Add this mixture to the cake batter and mix until well incorporated.

Divide and Bake:

Divide the cake batter evenly between the prepared cake pans. Smooth the tops.

Bake:

Bake in the preheated oven for 25-30 minutes or until a toothpick inserted into the center of the cakes comes out clean.

Cool:

Allow the cakes to cool in the pans for about 10 minutes, then transfer them to a wire rack to cool completely.

For Cream Cheese Frosting:

Cream Cheese and Butter:

In a mixing bowl, beat the softened cream cheese and unsalted butter until smooth and creamy.

Add Sugar and Vanilla:

Gradually add the powdered sugar and vanilla extract, beating until the frosting is smooth and fluffy.

Assemble and Decorate:

Frost the Cake:

Once the cakes are completely cooled, spread a layer of cream cheese frosting on top of one cake layer. Place the second cake layer on top and frost the entire cake with the remaining frosting.

Decorate:

Optionally, decorate the cake with chopped pecans or walnuts around the edges and fresh raspberries or strawberries on top.

Serve:

Slice and serve your Decadent Red Velvet Cake, savoring every bite of its rich, moist, and delicious layers.

<u>**Tips:**</u>

- Adjust the amount of red food coloring to achieve your desired shade of red.

- Allow the cakes to cool completely before frosting to prevent the frosting from melting.

- Refrigerate the cake if not serving immediately, and let it sit at room temperature for a while before serving to enhance the flavors and texture.

- Customize the cake's decoration with your favorite toppings, such as chocolate shavings or edible flowers.

Enjoy the sumptuous delight of Decadent Red Velvet Cake, a classic dessert that's sure to impress your family and guests!

11. Fresh Strawberry Cheesecake

Fresh Strawberry Cheesecake

Fresh Strawberry Cheesecake is a delightful dessert that combines the creamy richness of cheesecake with the bright and refreshing taste of fresh strawberries. With a buttery graham cracker crust, velvety cheesecake filling, and a vibrant strawberry topping, this dessert is a perfect treat for any occasion.

Ingredients:

For the Strawberry Cheesecake:

- 1+1/2 cups graham cracker crumbs
- 1/2 cup unsalted butter (melted)
- 3 (8-ounce) packages cream cheese (softened)
- 1 cup granulated sugar
- 3 large eggs
- 1 teaspoon vanilla extract
- 2 cups fresh strawberries (hulled and chopped)
- 1 tablespoon all-purpose flour
- 1/2 cup sour cream
- 1/4 cup strawberry jam (optional, for glazing)

Optional Ingredients:

- Additional fresh strawberries for garnish

Step-by-Step Instructions:

For the Strawberry Cheesecake:

Preheat the Oven:

Preheat your oven to 325°F (160°C). Grease a 9-inch springform pan.

Prepare the Crust:

In a mixing bowl, combine the graham cracker crumbs and melted butter. Press the mixture firmly into the bottom of the prepared pan to create the crust.

Beat Cream Cheese and Sugar:

In a large mixing bowl, beat the softened cream cheese and granulated sugar until smooth and creamy.

Add Eggs and Vanilla:

Add the eggs one at a time, mixing well after each addition. Stir in the vanilla extract.

Toss Strawberries in Flour:

In a separate bowl, gently toss the chopped strawberries with 1 tablespoon of all-purpose flour. This helps prevent them from sinking to the bottom of the cheesecake.

- Whipped cream for serving

Suggested Pairings:

- A glass of sparkling wine or champagne for a touch of elegance
- Fresh mint leaves or chocolate shavings for extra garnish.

Add Strawberry and Sour Cream:

Fold the floured strawberries into the cream cheese mixture, followed by the sour cream. Mix until well combined.

Pour Over Crust:

Pour the cheesecake filling over the prepared graham cracker crust in the pan.

Bake:

Bake the cheesecake in the preheated oven for 45-55 minutes, or until the edges are set, and the center is slightly jiggly.

Cool and Chill:

Allow the cheesecake to cool in the oven with the door ajar for about an hour. Then, refrigerate it for at least 4 hours or overnight to set.

For Glazing (Optional):

Heat Strawberry Jam:

If desired, heat the strawberry jam in a small saucepan over low heat until it becomes liquid.

Glaze the Cheesecake:

Once the cheesecake is fully chilled, spread the optional strawberry jam glaze over the top.
Decorate and Serve:

Garnish:

Optionally, garnish the fresh strawberry cheesecake with additional fresh strawberries, whipped cream, fresh mint leaves, or chocolate shavings.

Slice and Serve:

Slice and serve your Fresh Strawberry Cheesecake, reveling in the creamy goodness and vibrant strawberry flavor.

<u>Tips:</u>

- Use room temperature cream cheese to ensure a smooth and creamy filling.

- Avoid overmixing the cheesecake batter to prevent cracking during baking.

- Allow the cheesecake to cool gradually to prevent cracks; the gradual cooling in the oven helps with this.

- Customize the glaze with other fruit jams or preserves if you prefer different flavors.

- Serve chilled for the best texture and flavor.

Enjoy your Fresh Strawberry Cheesecake, a delectable dessert that captures the essence of summer in every bite!

12. Homemade Chocolate Truffles

Homemade Chocolate Truffles

<u>**Introduction to the Dish:**</u>

Homemade Chocolate Truffles are a luxurious treat that combines the smoothness of rich dark chocolate with the creamy indulgence of ganache. These bite-sized delights are a perfect gift or a delightful addition to any dessert spread.

Ingredients:

For Homemade Chocolate Truffles:

- 8 ounces (about 1 1/2 cups) high-quality dark chocolate (70% cocoa or higher), finely chopped
- 1/2 cup heavy cream
- 2 tablespoons unsalted butter, at room temperature
- 1 teaspoon pure vanilla extract
- A pinch of salt

For Coating:

- Cocoa powder
- Finely chopped nuts (such as almonds, hazelnuts, or pistachios)
- Shredded coconut
- Confectioners' sugar
- Melted chocolate (for dipping)

Optional Ingredients:

Step-by-Step Instructions:

Chop the Chocolate:

Finely chop the high-quality dark chocolate and place it in a heatproof bowl.

Heat the Cream:

In a saucepan, heat the heavy cream over medium heat until it just begins to simmer. Remove it from the heat immediately.

Create the Ganache:

- Pour the hot cream over the chopped chocolate. Let it sit for a minute to soften the chocolate.
- Gently stir the mixture until the chocolate is completely melted and the ganache is smooth and shiny.

Add Butter and Flavor:

Stir in the unsalted butter, pure vanilla extract, and a pinch of salt. Mix until the butter is fully incorporated.

Optional Liqueur:

If using, add a splash of liqueur to the ganache and mix until combined.

Chill the Ganache:

- A splash of liqueur (such as Grand Marnier, Amaretto, or Kahlúa) for flavor variation

Suggested Pairings:

- A glass of red wine or a cup of coffee to complement the chocolatey richness
- Fresh berries or dried fruits for a sweet contrast

Cover the ganache with plastic wrap, making sure it touches the surface to prevent a skin from forming. Refrigerate for at least 2-3 hours or until firm.

Shape the Truffles:

- Once the ganache is firm, use a spoon or a melon baller to scoop out portions of the ganache.
- Roll each portion between your palms to form small, round truffles. Place them on a parchment paper-lined tray.

Coat the Truffles:

Roll the truffles in cocoa powder, finely chopped nuts, shredded coconut, confectioners' sugar, or dip them in melted chocolate for a decorative coating.

Chill Again:

Place the coated truffles in the refrigerator for about 30 minutes to set.

<u>Tips:</u>

- Use high-quality dark chocolate for the best flavor and texture.

- Customize your truffles by adding your favorite liqueur or extract for unique flavors.

- Be creative with coatings; try a variety of options to suit your taste.

- Work quickly when shaping the truffles to prevent them from melting in your hands.

- Store the finished truffles in an airtight container in the refrigerator for longer shelf life.

Enjoy the delightful decadence of Homemade Chocolate Truffles, a bite-sized piece of chocolate heaven!

Comfort Food Classics

Greek Mezze Feast

Spanish Paella Perfection

Hearty Beef Stew

Vegan Sushi Rolls

Plant-Based Chocolate Mousse

Persian Rice Pilaf

13. Greek Mezze Feast

Greek Mezze Feast

Introduction to the Dish:

A Greek Mezze Feast is a delightful and communal way to savor the vibrant flavors of Mediterranean cuisine. This spread of small, flavorful dishes offers a diverse and satisfying dining experience, perfect for sharing with family and friends.

Ingredients:

For Greek Mezze Feast:

- Hummus
- Tzatziki sauce
- Greek salad (cucumbers, tomatoes, red onions, Kalamata olives, and feta cheese)
- Spanakopita (spinach and feta pastry)
- Dolmades (stuffed grape leaves)
- Falafel
- Taramasalata (fish roe dip)
- Pita bread or flatbread
- Grilled or marinated chicken or lamb (optional)
- Lemon wedges and fresh herbs for garnish

Optional Ingredients:

Step-by-Step Instructions:

Prepare the Mezze Dishes:

Prepare or acquire classic Greek mezze dishes such as hummus, tzatziki sauce, Greek salad, spanakopita, dolmades, falafel, and taramasalata. You can also include grilled or marinated chicken or lamb as a protein option.

Serve Fresh Bread:

Warm pita bread or flatbread and serve it alongside the mezze dishes.

Garnish and Presentation:

Garnish the dishes with lemon wedges and fresh herbs like mint and parsley for a beautiful presentation.

Optional Additions:

Consider adding skordalia (garlic potato dip), melitzanosalata (eggplant dip), Greek-style roasted vegetables, or baklava for dessert to enhance the feast.

Pair with Beverages:

- Skordalia (garlic potato dip)
- Melitzanosalata (eggplant dip)
- Greek-style roasted vegetables
- Baklava for dessert

Suggested Pairings:

- A crisp white wine, such as Assyrtiko, or a Greek beer like Mythos
- A Mediterranean-style fruit salad with citrus and honey for dessert

Serve with a crisp white wine, a Greek beer, or traditional ouzo, if desired.

Serve and Enjoy:

Arrange the mezze dishes on a large platter or individual plates, allowing everyone to choose their favorites. Encourage guests to scoop, dip, and enjoy the array of flavors.

Tips:

- Use fresh and quality ingredients to create authentic and flavorful mezze dishes.

- Experiment with various dips, spreads, and proteins to cater to different preferences.

- Include a variety of textures and flavors, such as creamy dips, crunchy falafel, and tangy salads.

- Offer a mix of hot and cold dishes for contrast and balance.

- Customize the feast to accommodate dietary preferences, such as vegetarian or vegan options.

Delight in the Mediterranean charm of a Greek Mezze Feast, where the vibrant flavors and communal spirit come together for a memorable dining experience!

14. Spanish Paella Perfection

Spanish Paella Perfection

Spanish Paella Perfection is a beloved dish that showcases the vibrant and robust flavors of Spain. This one-pan wonder features a delightful mix of saffron-infused rice, succulent seafood, flavorful chorizo, and a medley of vegetables, all cooked to aromatic perfection.

Ingredients:

For Spanish Paella Perfection:

- 2 cups bomba rice or short-grain Spanish rice
- 4 cups chicken or vegetable broth (hot)
- 1/2 cup dry white wine (optional)
- 1 pound boneless chicken thighs (cut into bite-sized pieces)
- 1/2 pound large shrimp (peeled and deveined)
- 1/2 pound mussels or clams (cleaned and scrubbed)
- 1/2 cup Spanish chorizo (sliced)
- 1 onion (chopped)
- 1 red bell pepper (sliced)
- 1 yellow bell pepper (sliced)
- 1 cup green beans (trimmed and halved)
- 4 cloves garlic (minced)

Step-by-Step Instructions:

Sear the Proteins:

In a large paella pan or wide skillet, heat olive oil over medium-high heat. Add the chicken pieces and shrimp. Season with salt, pepper, and smoked paprika. Sear until chicken is browned and shrimp turn pink. Remove and set aside.

Sauté the Aromatics:

In the same pan, add more olive oil if needed. Sauté the onions, garlic, and bell peppers until softened.

Add Chorizo and Spices:

Stir in the Spanish chorizo slices and continue to cook until they release their flavorful oils. Sprinkle in the ground turmeric and saffron threads with their soaking water.

Toast the Rice:

Add the bomba rice to the pan and stir to coat it in the flavorful mixture. Toast the rice for a minute or two.

Pour in Wine and Broth:

If using wine, pour it into the pan and let it simmer for a few minutes until it reduces slightly. Then, add the hot chicken or vegetable broth.

- 1 teaspoon saffron threads (soaked in 2 tablespoons hot water)
- 1 teaspoon smoked paprika (pimentón)
- 1/2 teaspoon ground turmeric
- Salt and freshly ground black pepper to taste
- Olive oil for cooking
- Fresh lemon wedges for serving
- Fresh parsley or cilantro leaves for garnish

Optional Ingredients:

- Artichoke hearts, roasted red peppers, or green peas
- Squid or octopus for a seafood medley
- Lobster tails or crayfish for a luxurious touch

Suggested Pairings:

- A Spanish red wine, such as Tempranillo, or a light and crisp Albariño
- A side of crusty bread with aioli for dipping
- Spanish flan or churros with chocolate sauce for dessert

Layer Ingredients:

Arrange the seared chicken, shrimp, mussels or clams, and any optional ingredients on top of the rice. Place them evenly across the pan.

Simmer and Cover:

Reduce the heat to medium-low and cover the paella with a lid or aluminum foil. Let it simmer for about 15-20 minutes, or until the rice is tender and has absorbed the liquid.

Check for Doneness:

When the rice is done, the paella should have a nice crust on the bottom, known as "socarrat." Listen for a faint crackling sound.

Garnish and Serve:

Remove from heat and let it rest for a few minutes. Garnish with fresh parsley or cilantro leaves and serve with lemon wedges.

Tips:

- Use a wide, shallow pan or a traditional paella pan for even cooking and the desired socarrat.

- Customize the ingredients to suit your preferences, but maintain the balance of flavors.

- Don't stir the paella once the broth is added; this helps create the socarrat.

- Adjust the cooking time as needed, as it can vary depending on your stovetop and pan.

Indulge in the flavors of Spain with Spanish Paella Perfection, a delightful dish that captures the essence of Spanish cuisine in every bite!

15. Hearty Beef Stew

Hearty Beef Stew

Introduction to the Dish:

Hearty Beef Stew is the epitome of comfort food, offering tender chunks of beef simmered in a flavorful broth with an array of vegetables and aromatic herbs. This dish warms the soul and satisfies even the heartiest appetite.

Ingredients:

For Hearty Beef Stew:

- 2 pounds beef stew meat, cut into 1-inch cubes
- 2 tablespoons vegetable oil
- 1 large onion, chopped
- 2 cloves garlic, minced
- 4 cups beef broth
- 1 cup red wine (optional)
- 2 bay leaves
- 1 teaspoon dried thyme
- 1 teaspoon dried rosemary
- 4 carrots, peeled and sliced
- 4 potatoes, peeled and diced
- 2 cups sliced celery
- 1 cup frozen peas
- Salt and freshly ground black pepper to taste

Step-by-Step Instructions:

Brown the Beef:

In a large, heavy-bottomed pot or Dutch oven, heat the vegetable oil over medium-high heat. Add the beef cubes and brown them on all sides. Remove and set aside.

Sauté the Aromatics:

In the same pot, add chopped onions and minced garlic. Sauté until they become fragrant and translucent.

Deglaze with Wine (Optional):

If using red wine, pour it into the pot to deglaze, scraping up any browned bits from the bottom of the pot. Simmer for a few minutes to reduce slightly.

Add Broth and Herbs:

Return the browned beef to the pot. Pour in the beef broth and add bay leaves, dried thyme, and dried rosemary. Season with salt and freshly ground black pepper to taste.

Simmer and Tenderize:

Cover the pot, reduce the heat to low, and let the stew simmer for about 1.5 to 2 hours, or until the beef is tender.

Add Vegetables:

Optional Ingredients:

- Mushrooms, or pearl onions for added depth of flavor
- A splash of Worcestershire sauce for richness

Suggested Pairings:

- A hearty crusty bread or dinner rolls for dipping
- A green salad or steamed greens for a balanced meal
- A glass of red wine or a dark beer for adults

Add carrots, potatoes, celery, and any optional ingredients (such as mushrooms or pearl onions) to the pot. Continue to simmer for an additional 30 minutes, or until the vegetables are tender.

Final Touch:

Stir in the frozen peas during the last few minutes of cooking until they are heated through.

Serve and Enjoy:

Remove the bay leaves and discard them. Ladle the hearty beef stew into bowls and serve hot.

<u>Tips:</u>

- Use beef stew meat that is well-marbled for a rich and tender stew.

- Feel free to customize the vegetables based on your preferences.

- The red wine adds depth to the flavor, but it can be omitted if preferred.

- Allow the stew to simmer low and slow for the best results, as this tenderizes the beef and enhances the flavors.

Savor the comforting flavors of Hearty Beef Stew, a wholesome and satisfying dish perfect for a cozy meal with loved ones.

Vegan Sushi Rolls

Introduction to the Dish:

Vegan Sushi Rolls offer a delightful twist on traditional sushi, making it accessible to those who follow a plant-based diet. These rolls feature a combination of seasoned sushi rice, fresh vegetables, and optional protein for a healthy and satisfying meal.

Ingredients:

For Vegan Sushi Rolls:

- 2 cups sushi rice
- 4 cups water
- 1/2 cup rice vinegar
- 2 tablespoons sugar
- 1 teaspoon salt
- Nori seaweed sheets
- Assorted vegetables (e.g., cucumber, carrot, avocado, bell pepper, and radish), thinly sliced or julienned
- Extra-firm tofu or tempeh, thinly sliced and pan-fried (optional protein)
- Soy sauce or tamari, for dipping
- Pickled ginger, for serving
- Wasabi paste, for serving
- Toasted sesame seeds, for garnish

Step-by-Step Instructions:

Prepare Sushi Rice:

Rinse the sushi rice under cold water until the water runs clear. Cook the rice according to package instructions. Once cooked, transfer the rice to a large bowl.

Season the Rice:

In a small saucepan, heat the rice vinegar, sugar, and salt over low heat, stirring until the sugar and salt dissolve. Pour the mixture over the cooked rice and gently fold it in to combine. Let the seasoned rice cool to room temperature.

Assemble the Sushi Rolls:

- Lay a bamboo sushi rolling mat on a clean surface and cover it with plastic wrap.
- Place a sheet of nori seaweed, shiny side down, on the bamboo mat.
- Wet your hands to prevent the rice from sticking, then evenly spread a layer of seasoned sushi rice over the nori, leaving a 1-inch border at the top.
- Arrange your choice of thinly sliced vegetables and optional protein in the center of the rice.

Roll and Shape:

Optional Ingredients:

- Sesame oil for drizzling on the rice
- Vegan mayonnaise or sriracha for added flavor
- Marinated mushrooms or sautéed mushrooms for variety

Suggested Pairings:

- A side of miso soup for a traditional Japanese experience
- A Japanese green tea or a refreshing cucumber-infused water

- Carefully lift the bamboo mat and the edge of the nori closest to you. Begin rolling away from you while applying gentle pressure to shape the roll.
- Continue rolling until you reach the exposed border of nori. Wet the border with a little water to seal the roll.

Slice and Serve:

Use a sharp, wet knife to slice the sushi roll into bite-sized pieces. Wipe the knife clean between cuts for neat slices.

Garnish and Serve:

- Arrange the vegan sushi rolls on a platter. Sprinkle with toasted sesame seeds for garnish.
- Serve with soy sauce or tamari, pickled ginger, and wasabi paste.

<u>Tips:</u>

- Use a sushi mat to help with rolling, but if you don't have one, you can also use a clean kitchen towel.

- Customize the filling with your favorite vegetables and protein sources.

- Dip your fingers in a mixture of water and rice vinegar when handling the rice to prevent sticking.

- Experiment with different sauces and condiments for added flavor.

Enjoy your Vegan Sushi Rolls, a plant-based delight that captures the essence of Japanese cuisine in every bite!

17. Plant-Based Chocolate Mousse

Plant-Based Chocolate Mousse

Introduction to the Dish:

Plant-Based Chocolate Mousse is a luscious and guilt-free dessert that transforms ripe avocados into a creamy and chocolatey indulgence. This dairy-free and vegan-friendly mousse is a delightful way to satisfy your sweet tooth.

Ingredients:

For Plant-Based Chocolate Mousse:

- 2 ripe avocados, peeled and pitted
- 1/2 cup unsweetened cocoa powder
- 1/2 cup pure maple syrup or agave nectar
- 1/4 cup almond milk or any plant-based milk of choice
- 1 teaspoon vanilla extract
- A pinch of salt

Optional Ingredients:

- 1-2 tablespoons peanut butter or almond butter for added creaminess
- Vegan whipped cream or coconut whipped cream for topping
- Fresh berries, sliced bananas, or chopped nuts for garnish

Step-by-Step Instructions:

Blend the Base:

In a food processor or blender, combine the ripe avocados, unsweetened cocoa powder, pure maple syrup or agave nectar, almond milk, vanilla extract, and a pinch of salt.

Blend Until Smooth:

Blend the ingredients until the mixture is smooth and creamy. Scrape down the sides of the bowl or blender as needed to ensure everything is well combined.

Adjust Sweetness:

Taste the chocolate mousse and adjust the sweetness by adding more maple syrup or agave nectar if desired.

Optional Creaminess:

For extra creaminess and a nutty flavor, you can add 1-2 tablespoons of peanut butter or almond butter to the mixture and blend again until smooth.

Chill and Serve:

Transfer the chocolate mousse to serving glasses or bowls. Cover and refrigerate for at least 1-2 hours to allow it to firm up and chill.

- A warm cup of herbal tea or a rich cup of coffee for a cozy treat
- A sprinkle of shaved chocolate or cocoa nibs for added texture

When ready to serve, garnish the plant-based chocolate mousse with vegan whipped cream, coconut whipped cream, or a sprinkle of shaved chocolate, and add fresh berries, sliced bananas, or chopped nuts for an extra touch of flavor and texture.

Tips:

- Use ripe avocados for the creamiest texture and subtle avocado flavor.

- Adjust the sweetness to your taste by adding more sweetener as needed.

- Experiment with different garnishes and toppings to customize your dessert.

- Serve the mousse chilled for the best taste and texture.

Indulge in the rich and velvety goodness of Plant-Based Chocolate Mousse, a delightful treat that's both satisfying and guilt-free.

18. Persian Rice Pilaf

Persian Rice Pilaf

Persian Rice Pilaf, known for its fragrant and fluffy grains, is a beloved dish in Iranian cuisine. It's an aromatic rice dish often served with a crispy layer of tahdig, making it a delightful addition to any meal.

Ingredients:

For Persian Rice Pilaf:

- 2 cups Basmati rice
- 4 cups water
- 2 tablespoons vegetable oil or butter
- 1 onion, finely chopped
- 1/2 teaspoon ground cumin
- 1/2 teaspoon ground cinnamon
- 1/2 cup slivered almonds or chopped pistachios
- 1/2 cup dried barberries or currants (optional)
- Salt and freshly ground black pepper to taste
- Saffron threads (a pinch), soaked in 2 tablespoons hot water
- Thin lavash bread or a tortilla (optional for crispy tahdig)

Optional Ingredients:

- Saffron-infused rice with crispy tahdig for added flavor and texture

Step-by-Step Instructions:

Rinse and Soak the Rice:

Rinse the Basmati rice in cold water until the water runs clear. Place the rice in a large bowl and cover it with cold water. Let it soak for at least 30 minutes.

Prepare the Saffron:

In a small bowl, soak a pinch of saffron threads in 2 tablespoons of hot water. Let it steep to create saffron-infused water.

Sauté the Onion and Spices:

In a large pot, heat the vegetable oil or butter over medium heat. Add finely chopped onions and sauté until they become translucent and golden brown.

Add Spices and Nuts:

Stir in ground cumin and ground cinnamon, cooking for about a minute until fragrant. Add slivered almonds or chopped pistachios, sautéing until they turn lightly golden.

Drain and Parboil the Rice:

Drain the soaked rice and add it to the pot. Stir gently to combine with the onions and spices. Add salt and freshly ground black pepper to taste. Pour in 4 cups of water and bring the mixture to a boil.

- A sprinkle of ground cardamom for aromatic depth

Suggested Pairings:

- A cucumber and tomato salad or a fresh herb salad for a refreshing side dish
- Yogurt-based sauces, such as cucumber yogurt or mast-o-khiar, for dipping
- A glass of traditional Persian tea or a cooling rosewater and mint drink

Cook and Steam:

Reduce the heat to low, cover the pot with a tight-fitting lid, and let the rice simmer for about 20-25 minutes, or until it's tender but still slightly al dente.

Saffron Infusion:

Drizzle the saffron-infused water over the top of the partially cooked rice. Use a fork to gently create holes in the rice, allowing the saffron to infuse and create a beautiful golden color.

Crispy Tahdig (Optional):

To make crispy tahdig, place a thin lavash bread or tortilla at the bottom of the pot before adding the rice. This will create a crispy layer at the bottom.

Final Steam:

Cover the pot with a clean kitchen towel and a tight-fitting lid. Let the rice steam for an additional 30-40 minutes on very low heat, allowing the tahdig to crisp up and the rice to fully cook and fluff up.

Serve and Garnish:

Gently fluff the Persian Rice Pilaf with a fork, being careful not to disturb the tahdig if using. Transfer the rice to a serving platter, and garnish with dried barberries or currants, if desired.

<u>Tips:</u>

Use high-quality Basmati rice for the best results.

To achieve crispy tahdig, keep the heat very low during the final steaming stage.

You can substitute dried barberries or currants with raisins if desired.

Allow the rice to rest for a few minutes before serving to settle the flavors.

Enjoy the aromatic and flavorful Persian Rice Pilaf, a timeless dish that's perfect as a side or even as a main course.

PART II

Mastering the Secrets of Cooking Like a Pro

I.
Preparation Is Key

1.1 Selecting the Right Ingredients

Selecting the right ingredients is a fundamental step in cooking like a pro. The quality of your ingredients can make or break your dish, so it's essential to choose wisely. Here's a step-by-step guide to help you select the right ingredients:

Step 1: Define Your Recipe

- Before you start shopping for ingredients, know exactly what you plan to cook. Having a clear recipe in mind will guide your ingredient choices. Consider the type of cuisine, dish, and dietary restrictions if any.

Step 2: Make a Shopping List

- Once you have your recipe in mind, create a detailed shopping list. List all the ingredients required, including quantities. This will help you stay organized and ensure you don't forget anything.

Step 3: Freshness Matters

- When it comes to fruits, vegetables, meats, and seafood, freshness is crucial. Here's what to look for:

- Fruits and Vegetables: Choose produce that is firm, vibrant in color, and free of bruises or blemishes. Smell and touch can be good indicators of freshness.

- Meats: Look for meat that is bright red (for beef), pink (for pork), or pale pink (for poultry). Avoid meat with a strong or unpleasant odor.

- Seafood: Fresh seafood should have a clean, briny smell and firm, moist flesh. Avoid seafood that smells fishy or has a slimy texture.

Step 4: Check Expiry Dates

- For packaged goods, always check the expiry or "best by" dates. Ensure that the products you choose are well within their shelf life to maintain freshness and safety.

Step 5: Read Labels

- Pay attention to ingredient labels, especially if you have dietary restrictions or food allergies. Make sure the product doesn't contain any ingredients that you or your guests should avoid.

Step 6: Go Organic or Local (Optional)

- If possible and within your budget, consider buying organic or locally sourced ingredients. They often have better flavor and may be more environmentally friendly.

Step 7: Compare Prices

- Compare prices and quality among different brands and stores. Sometimes, store brands offer similar quality at a lower cost.

Step 8: Avoid Impulse Buys

- Stick to your shopping list and avoid impulse buys, especially if you're on a budget. Impulse purchases can lead to food waste.

Step 9: Consider Seasonality

- For fruits and vegetables, consider what's in season. Seasonal produce is often fresher, more flavorful, and less expensive.

Step 10: Adapt to Dietary Needs

- If you or your guests have specific dietary needs, such as vegetarian, vegan, gluten-free, or low-sodium, make sure to choose ingredients that align with those requirements.

By following these steps, you'll be well-equipped to select the right ingredients for your recipes. Remember that ingredient quality plays a significant role in the final taste and presentation of your dishes, so take your time and choose wisely.

Efficient food storage is a critical aspect of cooking like a pro. Properly storing your ingredients can help extend their freshness, reduce waste, and make meal preparation more convenient. Here's a step-by-step guide on how to efficiently store your food:

Step 1: Organize Your Storage Space

- Before you start storing food, ensure that your storage space is clean and well-organized. Remove any expired or spoiled items from your pantry, refrigerator, and freezer.

Step 2: Use Airtight Containers

- Invest in high-quality airtight containers for both dry and wet ingredients. These containers help prevent moisture and air from getting in, which can lead to food spoilage.

- For dry ingredients like grains, pasta, and cereals, use airtight containers to keep them fresh and protect them from pests.

- For leftovers or meal prep, use airtight containers to seal in the flavor and prevent odors from spreading.

Step 3: Label Everything

- Label containers with the date of purchase or preparation to keep track of freshness. Additionally, label ingredients that look similar to avoid confusion.

- Use a marker or adhesive labels that can be easily removed or replaced.

Step 4: Store Raw and Cooked Foods Separately

- To prevent cross-contamination, store raw meats, poultry, and seafood separately from cooked foods and fresh produce.

- Use separate containers or storage areas for raw and cooked items to reduce the risk of foodborne illnesses.

Step 5: Optimize Refrigerator Storage

- In the refrigerator, keep perishable items like dairy, eggs, and fresh produce on the shelves, not in the door. The door is the warmest part of the fridge and is best for items with longer shelf lives.

- Use clear containers or bins to group similar items together, making it easier to find what you need.

Step 6: Properly Freeze Foods

- When freezing foods, use airtight freezer bags or containers to prevent freezer burn and maintain quality.

- Remove as much air as possible from freezer bags to minimize ice crystals.

- Label frozen items with the date and description for quick identification.

Step 7: Rotate Your Stock

- Practice the "first in, first out" (FIFO) method to ensure that older items are used before newer ones. This helps reduce food waste.

Step 8: Be Mindful of Temperature

- Ensure that your refrigerator and freezer are set to the appropriate temperatures to keep food safe.

- Refrigerator: Keep it at or below 40°F (4°C).

- Freezer: Maintain a temperature of 0°F (-18°C) or lower.

Step 9: Check for Spoilage

- Regularly inspect your stored ingredients for signs of spoilage, such as mold, off smells, or unusual texture. Dispose of any spoiled items promptly.

- Plan your meals in advance and organize your storage accordingly. This will help you use ingredients before they expire and minimize food waste.

By following these steps, you can efficiently store your food, ensuring that your ingredients remain fresh and safe for longer periods. This not only contributes to cooking like a pro but also helps you save money and reduce food waste.

Having the right kitchen tools is paramount when it comes to cooking like a pro. The following is a comprehensive list of essential kitchen tools, along with step-by-step guidance on their selection and usage, complemented by practical examples:

1. Chef's Knife

- **Selection:** Choose a high-quality, sharp chef's knife with a comfortable handle. The blade should be around 8-10 inches in length for versatility.

- **Usage:** The chef's knife is your go-to tool for chopping, slicing, and dicing. For example, when making a vegetable stir-fry, use it to quickly and precisely chop a variety of vegetables.

2. Cutting Board

- **Selection:** Opt for a large, sturdy cutting board made of wood or plastic. Wooden boards are durable and gentle on knife blades.

- **Usage:** Place the cutting board on your countertop, providing a clean and safe surface for chopping, slicing, and other food preparation tasks. For instance, use it to chop herbs when making a fresh salad.

3. Paring Knife

- **Selection:** Choose a small, sharp paring knife with a pointed blade. It's ideal for intricate tasks.

- **Usage:** Use the paring knife for peeling and trimming fruits and vegetables. For example, when preparing a fruit platter, use it to peel and slice apples.

4. Tongs

- **Selection:** Look for tongs with a locking mechanism and heat-resistant grips for safety.

- **Usage:** Tongs are versatile for flipping, tossing, and serving. When grilling chicken, use tongs to turn the pieces for even cooking.

5. Mixing Bowls

- **Selection:** Invest in a set of mixing bowls in various sizes, preferably with lids for storage.

- **Usage:** Mixing bowls are essential for combining ingredients, marinating meats, and tossing salads. For instance, use a mixing bowl to whisk together dressing ingredients for a Caesar salad.

6. Whisk

- **Selection:** Choose a whisk with wire loops for efficient mixing.

- **Usage:** Whisks are excellent for blending, beating, and emulsifying. When preparing pancake batter, use a whisk to ensure a smooth, lump-free consistency.

7. Measuring Cups and Spoons

- **Selection:** Get a set of measuring cups and spoons made of durable materials for precise measurements.

- **Usage:** Measuring cups and spoons are essential for accurate portioning of ingredients. When baking chocolate chip cookies, use them to measure flour, sugar, and chocolate chips.

8. Wooden Spoon

- **Selection:** Select a wooden spoon with a comfortable grip and smooth finish.

- **Usage:** Wooden spoons are great for stirring and sautéing. When making a hearty soup, use a wooden spoon to stir the ingredients and prevent sticking.

9. Microplane Grater

- **Selection:** Choose a fine-grain microplane grater for zesting citrus, grating hard cheeses, and spices.

- **Usage:** Microplane graters are perfect for adding zest to dishes. When making a lemon-infused pasta, use it to zest lemon peel.

- **Selection:** Invest in a variety of baking sheets, cake pans, and roasting pans made of quality materials.

- **Usage:** These are essential for baking and roasting. When preparing a roast chicken, use a roasting pan to achieve crispy, golden skin.

Having these essential kitchen tools and knowing how to use them effectively will elevate your cooking skills and make your culinary endeavors more enjoyable and efficient. They are the building blocks for mastering the secrets of cooking like a professional chef.

II.
Mastering Basic Techniques

2.1 Proper Knife Skills

Mastering proper knife skills is a fundamental aspect of cooking like a professional chef. Precise cutting techniques not only enhance the presentation of your dishes but also improve the overall cooking experience. Here's a step-by-step guide on developing proper knife skills with practical examples:

Step 1: Choose the Right Knife

- **Selection**: Select the appropriate knife for the task at hand. For example:

  - Chef's Knife: Ideal for chopping, slicing, and dicing.

  - Paring Knife: Suitable for intricate tasks like peeling and trimming.

  - Bread Knife: Designed for slicing bread without crushing it.

Step 2: Maintain Sharp Blades

- **Maintenance:** Keep your knives sharp by regularly honing and sharpening them. Dull knives are more dangerous and less effective.

  - **Honing:** Use a honing rod or sharpening stone to straighten the blade's edge.

  - **Sharpening**: Use a knife sharpener or have your knives professionally sharpened when needed.

Step 3: Grip and Stance

- **Grip**: Hold the knife with a firm but not overly tight grip, using your dominant hand.

- Stance: Stand with your feet shoulder-width apart and maintain a comfortable posture. Keep your non-dominant hand (known as the "guide hand") in a claw-like shape to hold and guide the food.

Step 4: Master Basic Cuts

- **Chopping:** To chop vegetables, start with a claw grip on the food, using your guide hand to guide the knife blade while your dominant hand applies downward pressure.

  - Example: When making a stir-fry, use a chopping motion to cut bell peppers into even strips.

- **Slicing:** For thin, uniform slices, maintain a smooth and consistent motion. Use your guide hand to control the thickness of the slices.

  - Example: When preparing a cucumber salad, slice the cucumbers thinly for a delicate texture.

- **Dicing:** To dice vegetables, make a series of evenly spaced vertical and horizontal cuts while maintaining the claw grip.

  - Example: When making a tomato salsa, dice tomatoes into small, uniform pieces.

Step 5: Practice Safe Cutting Techniques

- **Finger Placement:** Always keep your fingers tucked behind your guide hand's knuckles to prevent accidental cuts.

- **Cut Away from Yourself:** When cutting, direct the knife blade away from your body to avoid injury.

- **Use a Cutting Board:** Place the cutting board on a stable surface to provide a safe and clean workspace.

Step 6: Proper Knife Care

- Cleaning: Wash knives immediately after use with mild detergent and warm water. Avoid abrasive scouring pads.

- Storage: Store knives in a knife block, magnetic strip, or blade guards to protect the blades and prevent accidents.

Step 7: Build Speed and Precision

- **Practice:** As with any skill, practice is key to improvement. Start with simple tasks and gradually work your way up to more complex cuts.

- **Efficiency:** Over time, you'll develop the speed and precision needed to efficiently prepare ingredients, like a professional chef.

Proper knife skills are essential in various culinary applications, from chopping vegetables for stir-fries to slicing meats for roasts. Mastering these techniques not only enhances your cooking but also ensures safety in the kitchen. Practice and patience are key to becoming proficient in handling knives like a pro.

Pressure cooking is a versatile and efficient cooking technique that can significantly speed up the cooking process while retaining the flavors and nutrients in your dishes. This section provides a detailed step-by-step guide on pressure cooking methods, along with practical examples to illustrate the process.

Step 1: Choose the Right Pressure Cooker

- **Selection:** Select a high-quality pressure cooker that suits your needs. There are stovetop and electric pressure cookers available. Ensure that it has safety features, such as pressure release valves and locking mechanisms.

Step 2: Familiarize Yourself with the Pressure Cooker Components

- **Components:** Get to know the essential components of a pressure cooker, including the lid, gasket, pressure release valve, and cooking pot.

Step 3: Read the Recipe Carefully

- **Recipe:** Start with a pressure cooker recipe that you'd like to try. Carefully read and understand the recipe instructions before you begin.

Step 4: Prepare Ingredients

- **Ingredients:** Prepare all the ingredients required for your dish, such as meats, vegetables, and liquids, according to the recipe's specifications.

Step 5: Assemble the Pressure Cooker

- **Assembling**: Place the cooking pot inside the pressure cooker and add the ingredients as specified in the recipe. Be mindful not to overfill the cooker; leave some space for expansion.

Step 6: Close and Seal the Lid

- **Closing:** Make sure the pressure cooker's lid is properly aligned with the pot and close it securely. Ensure that the pressure release valve is in the sealing position.

Step 7: Set Cooking Time and Pressure

- **Setting:** Depending on your pressure cooker model and the recipe, set the cooking time and pressure level. High pressure is typically used for most recipes.

Step 8: Start Cooking

- **Initiating:** Place the pressure cooker on the stovetop or plug in your electric pressure cooker. Turn on the heat or select the appropriate cooking mode to start building pressure.

Step 9: Maintain and Monitor Pressure

- **Pressure Build-Up:** As the pressure builds inside the cooker, the steam will be trapped, raising the internal temperature. The pressure indicator will pop up when the desired pressure is reached.

- **Monitoring:** Maintain a steady temperature to keep the pressure constant. Adjust the heat if necessary.

Step 10: Release Pressure

- **Natural Release:** After cooking, allow the pressure to naturally release by turning off the heat and waiting for the pressure indicator to drop. This method is suitable for delicate foods like rice or custards.

- **Quick Release:** For foods that need to stop cooking immediately, use the quick-release method. Carefully turn the pressure release valve to release steam. Be cautious of hot steam.

Step 11: Open the Lid Safely

- **Opening:** Once the pressure is fully released and the pressure indicator is down, it's safe to open the lid. Open it away from your face to avoid the release of residual steam.

Step 12: Serve and Enjoy

   - **Serving:** Dish out your perfectly cooked meal and savor the flavors and tenderness achieved through pressure cooking.

Practical Example: Let's say you want to make a classic Beef Stew using a pressure cooker. You would assemble the ingredients (beef, vegetables, broth, and seasonings) in the cooker, set the cooking time and pressure as per the recipe (usually around 25-30 minutes at high pressure), and then follow the steps for pressure buildup, pressure release, and safe lid opening. The result is a hearty, tender beef stew in a fraction of the time it would take with traditional cooking methods.

Pressure cooking is a fantastic method for busy cooks and allows for the creation of delicious dishes in less time while preserving the quality of the ingredients. Mastering pressure cooking techniques opens up a world of culinary possibilities.

Searing and sautéing are two essential cooking techniques that can elevate the flavor and texture of your dishes. These methods are commonly used to prepare meats, vegetables, and even some seafood. In this guide, we'll break down the steps for each technique with clear instructions and practical examples.

Searing Technique:

Step 1: Choose the Right Pan

- **Selection:** Opt for a heavy-bottomed skillet or pan, preferably made of cast iron or stainless steel. These materials distribute heat evenly and allow for better browning.

Step 2: Preheat the Pan

- **Preheating:** Place the skillet over medium-high heat and allow it to become hot. You can test the readiness by sprinkling a few drops of water onto the pan. If they sizzle and evaporate quickly, it's ready.

Step 3: Prepare the Ingredient

- Preparation: Pat the meat (e.g., steak or chicken) dry with paper towels and season it with salt and pepper. For vegetables, make sure they are dry and sliced uniformly for even cooking.

Step 4: Add Oil

- **Oil:** Add a small amount of high-heat cooking oil to the hot skillet. Swirl it around to coat the pan evenly.

Step 5: Place the Ingredient in the Pan

- **Searing:** Carefully place the meat or vegetables into the hot pan. Avoid overcrowding to ensure even browning. Allow the ingredient to sear without moving it for a few minutes until a golden crust forms.

Step 6: Flip or Stir

- **Turning:** Once a crust has developed, flip the meat or stir the vegetables to sear the other side. Repeat until all sides are evenly browned.

Step 7: Finish Cooking

- **Completion:** Depending on the thickness and desired doneness, you may need to finish cooking in the pan or transfer the ingredient to an oven to achieve the desired internal temperature.

Practical Example: Imagine you're searing a bone-in ribeye steak. You preheat the skillet until it's hot, add a bit of oil, season the steak with salt and pepper, and place it in the pan. Let it sear without moving for a few minutes on each side until it reaches your preferred level of doneness. This will create a delicious crust on the steak.

Sautéing Technique:

Step 1: Choose the Right Pan

- **Selection:** Similar to searing, use a skillet or sauté pan with a wide cooking surface and a heavy bottom.

Step 2: Preheat the Pan and Add Oil

- **Preheating:** Heat the skillet over medium-high heat and add a small amount of oil.

Step 3: Prepare Ingredients

- **Preparation:** For sautéing vegetables, make sure they are clean and cut into uniform pieces. For proteins like chicken or shrimp, ensure they are dry and seasoned.

Step 4: Add Ingredients

- **Addition:** Place the ingredients into the hot pan. Start with items that take longer to cook (e.g., onions) and gradually add others, stirring frequently.

Step 5: Stir and Toss

- **Stirring:** Continuously stir or toss the ingredients to ensure even cooking and prevent sticking or burning.

Step 6: Finish Cooking

- **Completion:** Once the ingredients are cooked to your desired level, remove them from the pan promptly to avoid overcooking.

Practical Example: Suppose you're sautéing a mix of bell peppers, onions, and garlic for a fajita filling. You start by heating the pan, adding a bit of oil, and placing the sliced onions in first. After a minute or two, add the sliced bell peppers, and finally, toss in minced garlic. Keep stirring until the vegetables are tender and slightly caramelized.

Searing and sautéing are versatile techniques that can be applied to various ingredients, allowing you to create flavorful and beautifully textured dishes. Mastery of these techniques is a significant step toward cooking like a pro.

III.
Balancing Flavors in Every Dish

3.1 Creating Well-Balanced Menus

Creating well-balanced menus is a crucial skill for cooking like a pro. A well-thought-out menu not only ensures a variety of flavors and textures but also caters to the dietary preferences and nutritional needs of your guests. Here's a step-by-step guide on how to create well-balanced menus with practical examples:

Step 1: Define the Theme or Cuisine

- **Theme**: Start by deciding the theme or cuisine of your menu. Whether it's Italian, Asian, or a mix of various cuisines, having a theme helps you narrow down ingredient choices.

Step 2: Consider Dietary Preferences and Restrictions

- **Dietary Needs**: Take into account any dietary preferences or restrictions your guests may have, such as vegetarian, vegan, gluten-free, or allergies.

- **Example:** If you're hosting a dinner party and one guest is vegetarian, plan a menu that includes both meat and plant-based options, like a vegetable stir-fry alongside a chicken dish.

Step 3: Plan a Balanced Meal

- **Balance:** Aim for a well-rounded meal that includes a variety of flavors and textures. A typical balanced meal includes a protein source, vegetables, and a starch (e.g., rice, pasta, or bread).

- **Example:** For a balanced Italian menu, you could serve grilled chicken (protein), a side of roasted vegetables, and a pasta dish with garlic bread (starch).

Step 4: Complement Flavors and Textures

- **Flavor Pairing**: Choose dishes that complement each other in terms of flavor. For example, if you have a spicy main course, consider a cooling side dish like a cucumber salad.

- **Texture Variety**: Include a mix of textures, such as crispy, creamy, and crunchy, to add interest to the meal.

- **Example**: Pair a crispy fried fish with creamy mashed potatoes and a crunchy coleslaw for a delightful contrast.

Step 5: Balance Colors and Presentation

- **Color Harmony**: Consider the colors of the dishes to create an appealing visual presentation. Vibrant, colorful plates are more inviting.

- **Example**: A menu with a green salad, orange sweet potato mash, and brown roasted chicken offers a visually pleasing combination.

Step 6: Plan for Portion Sizes

- **Portion Control**: Estimate portion sizes to avoid over-serving or under-serving. Ensure that each course is appropriately portioned to prevent food waste.

- **Example:** For a multi-course meal, serve smaller portions of each course to allow guests to enjoy every dish without feeling overly full.

Step 7: Taste Test and Adjust

- **Testing:** Before the event, prepare and taste each dish to ensure that it meets your expectations in terms of flavor and presentation. Make adjustments if needed.

- **Example:** If you find that a sauce is too salty, adjust it by adding more of the other ingredients to balance the flavors.

Step 8: Plan for Timing

- **Timing:** Create a timeline for cooking and serving each course. Consider the cooking times and temperatures of different dishes to ensure they all come to the table at the right moment.

- **Example:** If you're preparing a four-course meal, plan to start cooking the main course early enough so that it's ready when your guests are seated.

Step 9: Offer Variety in Beverages

- **Beverages:** Don't forget about beverage options. Include a variety of drinks such as water, wine, cocktails, or non-alcoholic alternatives to complement the meal.

- **Example:** For a Mexican-themed menu, offer margaritas, agua fresca, and Mexican beer as beverage choices.

Step 10: Presentation Matters

- **Presentation:** Pay attention to plating and garnishing to make each dish visually appealing. A well-presented meal is more enjoyable.

- **Example:** Use fresh herbs, colorful sauces, or edible flowers as garnishes to enhance the presentation of your dishes.

By following these steps and considering the examples provided, you can create well-balanced menus that cater to various tastes and dietary preferences, ensuring a memorable dining experience for your guests.

Creating natural sauces is an essential skill for enhancing the flavors of your dishes. Natural sauces are made from scratch using fresh, whole ingredients, and they can elevate your culinary creations to a professional level. Here's a step-by-step guide on how to craft natural sauces with clear instructions and practical examples:

Step 1: Choose Your Base Ingredients

- **Selection**: Start by selecting the main ingredients for your sauce. Common bases include tomatoes, cream, broth, wine, or olive oil.

Step 2: Gather Your Ingredients

- **Ingredients**: Assemble all the necessary components for your sauce, including aromatics (onions, garlic, shallots), herbs (such as basil, thyme, or rosemary), and any additional flavor enhancers (e.g., mushrooms or capers).

Step 3: Prepare Your Ingredients

- **Preparation:** Chop, mince, or dice your ingredients as required by the recipe. This ensures even cooking and consistent flavor distribution.

- **Example**: For a classic tomato sauce, chop onions, mince garlic, and dice tomatoes.

Step 4: Heat Your Cooking Fat

- **Cooking Fat:** Heat a small amount of cooking fat, such as olive oil or butter, in a saucepan over medium heat.

Step 5: Sauté Aromatics and Herbs

- **Sautéing**: Add your chopped aromatics and herbs to the heated fat. Sauté them until they become fragrant and onions turn translucent.

- **Example**: In a mushroom cream sauce, you might sauté minced shallots and fresh thyme in butter until they are aromatic and tender.

Step 6: Deglaze with Liquid

- **Deglazing**: Pour in a liquid like wine, broth, or cream to deglaze the pan. Scrape the flavorful bits from the bottom of the pan and allow the liquid to reduce slightly.

- **Example:** When making a pan sauce for seared chicken, deglaze the pan with white wine and let it simmer until reduced by half.

Step 7: Add Main Ingredient

- **Main Ingredient**: Introduce your main ingredient (e.g., tomatoes for a tomato sauce or mushrooms for a mushroom sauce) to the pan. Simmer the sauce until the ingredient softens and melds with the flavors.

- **Example**: For a tomato sauce, add diced tomatoes and simmer until they break down into a rich, thick sauce.

Step 8: Season and Taste

- **Seasoning:** Season your sauce with salt, pepper, and any additional herbs or spices to taste. Regularly taste and adjust as needed.

- **Example**: A béchamel sauce might be seasoned with a pinch of nutmeg, salt, and white pepper.

Step 9: Finish and Thicken (if needed)

- **Thickening:** If your sauce needs thickening, you can add a roux (equal parts fat and flour), a cornstarch slurry, or reduce it further on low heat until it reaches the desired consistency.

- **Example:** To thicken a gravy sauce, add a roux and whisk until smooth.

Step 10: Strain (if desired)

- **Straining**: For a smoother sauce, you can strain it through a fine mesh strainer to remove any solids or impurities.

   - **Example:** A velouté sauce, which is part of the French mother sauces, is often strained for a silky texture.

Step 11: Serve and Enjoy

   - **Serving:** Once your natural sauce is ready, ladle it over your prepared dish, whether it's pasta, meat, or vegetables, and enjoy the enhanced flavors it brings to your meal.

Crafting natural sauces from scratch allows you to tailor the flavors to your liking and create dishes that truly stand out. With practice and experimentation, you can develop your sauce-making skills and become a more proficient home chef.

PART III

Serving Your Creations with Elegance

IV.
The Art of Plating

4.1 Plate Presentation Techniques

Plate presentation is a crucial aspect of culinary artistry, and it can elevate your dishes from ordinary to extraordinary. The way you arrange food on a plate not only affects the visual appeal but also influences the overall dining experience. Here's a step-by-step guide on plate presentation techniques with clear instructions and practical examples:

Step 1: Choose the Right Plate

- **Selection:** Start by selecting an appropriate plate or platter that complements your dish. The size, shape, and color of the plate should enhance the visual presentation.

- **Example**: For a delicate seafood dish, consider using a round, white plate to showcase the vibrant colors of the seafood and accompanying vegetables.

Step 2: Plan the Composition

- **Composition**: Visualize how you want to arrange the elements of your dish on the plate. Think about balance, symmetry, and the overall aesthetic.

- **Example:** If you're plating a salad, consider how you'll layer the greens, arrange the toppings, and drizzle the dressing for an appealing look.

Step 3: Start with the Main Element

- **Main Element**: Begin by placing the main element of the dish on the plate, typically in the center. This could be the protein (e.g., steak, fish, or tofu) or the main course.

- **Example:** For a grilled chicken breast with vegetables, position the chicken breast in the center of the plate.

Step 4: Use the Rule of Thirds

- **Rule of Thirds**: Divide the plate into three imaginary sections both horizontally and vertically. This helps with creating balanced and visually pleasing compositions.

- **Example**: When plating a pasta dish, you might place the main pasta portion in one-third of the plate and the accompanying sauce and garnish in the other two-thirds.

Step 5: Add Complementary Elements

- **Complementary Elements**: Arrange side dishes, vegetables, or garnishes around the main element. Consider color, texture, and height variations to create interest.

- **Example**: If serving a steak, you can add roasted asparagus and garlic mashed potatoes alongside, adding both color and variety to the plate.

Step 6: Mind the Negative Space

- **Negative Space**: Don't overcrowd the plate. Leave some empty space around the elements to allow each component to shine and prevent the plate from looking cluttered.

- **Example**: When plating a dessert like a chocolate lava cake, use a dusting of powdered sugar sparingly to create an elegant presentation.

Step 7: Garnish Thoughtfully

- **Garnishes:** Use fresh herbs, edible flowers, microgreens, or a drizzle of sauce as garnishes. Garnishes add visual appeal and can tie the elements together.

- **Example**: A sprinkle of chopped chives or a few basil leaves can enhance the visual appeal of a creamy soup.

Step 8: Maintain Clean Edges

- **Clean Edges**: Wipe any smudges or spills on the rim of the plate to ensure a clean presentation. A well-maintained plate looks more appetizing.

- **Example:** When serving a sauce-rich dish, use a paper towel to clean any excess sauce from the rim of the plate.

Step 9: Step Back and Assess

- **Assessment:** Step back and view the plate from a distance to evaluate the overall composition. Make any final adjustments if necessary.

- **Example:** Sometimes, stepping back allows you to see if there's a need for additional garnish or if the arrangement needs slight tweaking.

Step 10: Practice and Experiment

- **Practice:** Plate presentation is an art that improves with practice. Experiment with different plating styles, colors, and arrangements to discover what works best for your dishes and personal style.

Remember that plate presentation not only enhances the visual appeal but also affects the perception of taste. With practice and attention to detail, you can become skilled at creating visually stunning dishes that impress and delight your guests.

Serving your dishes with professionalism and finesse adds an extra layer of elegance to your culinary creations. It ensures that your guests not only enjoy the flavors but also appreciate the effort and attention to detail you've put into presenting the meal. Here's a step-by-step guide on professional serving tips with clear instructions and practical examples:

Step 1: Preparing the Table

- **Table Setting:** Begin by setting the dining table in an inviting and organized manner. Ensure that you have all the necessary utensils, glassware, and plates for each course.

Step 2: Timing is Key

- **Timing:** Coordinate the timing of your dishes to serve them at their best. Hot dishes should be served hot, and cold dishes should be served cold.

Step 3: Serving Tools

- **Appropriate Utensils**: Use the appropriate serving utensils for each dish. For example, use a fish spatula to delicately transfer a fillet of fish, and use tongs for salad greens.

Step 4: Announce the Dish

- **Announcement**: If you're serving multiple courses, announce each dish as you present it to the table. Provide a brief description of the dish to pique your guests' curiosity.

Step 5: Right-Hand Rule

- **Right-Hand Rule**: When serving or clearing plates, use the right-hand rule - approach from the guest's right side and serve from the left. When clearing, do the opposite.

Step 6: Serve from the Left, Remove from the Right

and removing from the right to avoid crossing over your guests.

Step 7: Maintain Proper Posture

- **Posture:** Maintain good posture when serving, with a straight back and a friendly, attentive demeanor. This adds professionalism to your service.

Step 8: Serve Individual Plates

- **Individual Plates**: Serve each guest's portion individually rather than placing a communal dish on the table. This adds a personal touch to the dining experience.

Step 9: Be Attentive to All Guests

- **Attention:** Be attentive to the needs of all guests at the table. Ensure everyone has been served before you start eating.

Step 10: Offer Condiments and Accompaniments

- **Condiments:** Offer condiments, sauces, or accompaniments separately so that guests can add them to their dishes according to their preferences.

- **Example**: If you're serving steak, provide a selection of sauces on the side, such as a peppercorn sauce or a chimichurri.

Step 11: Use a Tray or Serving Cart

- **Tray or Cart:** When serving multiple courses, consider using a tray or serving cart to transport dishes efficiently and maintain their temperature.

Step 12: Check for Allergies and Dietary Restrictions

- **Allergies**: Before serving, double-check with your guests if there are any allergies or dietary restrictions you should be aware of.

Step 13: Pace the Meal

- **Pacing**: Pace the meal appropriately, allowing guests time to savor each course without feeling rushed. Clear plates and dishes promptly when everyone has finished.

Step 14: Dessert Presentation

- **Dessert:** When serving dessert, use dessert forks and spoons, and present them attractively. Consider including a small dessert fork or spoon rest on the side.

Step 15: Coffee or Tea Service

- **Coffee/Tea:** Offer coffee or tea after the meal, along with sugar, cream, and any accompaniments. Use a coffee or tea service set for an elegant touch.

By following these professional serving tips, you can ensure that your guests have an enjoyable dining experience and appreciate the effort you've put into creating and presenting your culinary masterpieces.

V.
How to Savor a Full Meal

5.1 The Importance of Mindful Eating

Mindful eating is a practice that involves being fully present and attentive while consuming your food. It's not just about what you eat, but how you eat it. This practice can lead to a more enjoyable and healthy relationship with food. Here's a step-by-step guide explaining the importance of mindful eating with practical examples:

Step 1: Awareness of Your Meal

- **Pause**: Before you start eating, take a moment to pause and appreciate the meal in front of you. Notice the colors, textures, and aromas of your food.

- **Example**: As you sit down to enjoy a colorful salad, take a moment to appreciate the vibrant greens, ripe tomatoes, and crisp cucumbers on your plate.

Step 2: Engage Your Senses

- **Sensory Experience**: As you take your first bite, pay attention to the flavors and textures. Chew slowly and savor each bite.

- **Example:** When tasting a piece of chocolate, notice the initial sweetness, followed by the smooth, melting texture, and the lingering cocoa flavor.

Step 3: Eat Without Distractions

- **Distraction-Free**: Avoid distractions like television, smartphones, or work while eating. Focus solely on the meal in front of you.

- **Example**: Instead of scrolling through your phone, sit at the dining table with no distractions and fully engage with your meal.

Step 4: Listen to Your Body

- **Hunger Signals:** Pay attention to your body's hunger and fullness cues. Eat when you're hungry and stop when you're satisfied, not overly full.

- **Example:** When you feel satisfied during a meal, put your fork down and take a moment to assess if you're still hungry.

Step 5: Mindful Portion Control

- Portion **Awareness**: Be mindful of portion sizes and serve reasonable amounts. Use smaller plates and utensils to help with portion control.

- **Example:** If you're having pasta, use a smaller bowl to avoid overloading your plate with excessive portions.

Step 6: Appreciate Each Bite

- **Gratitude**: Express gratitude for your food and the effort that went into preparing it. This can enhance your overall dining experience.

- **Example**: Before starting your meal, silently express gratitude for the ingredients, the cook, and the meal itself.

Step 7: Slow Down

- **Pace Yourself**: Eat at a relaxed pace. Put your utensils down between bites, take sips of water, and engage in conversation if dining with others.

- **Example:** When enjoying a steak dinner, savor each bite by chewing slowly, appreciating the tenderness and flavor.

Step 8: Be Mindful of Emotional Eating

- **Emotional Awareness:** Recognize if you're eating due to emotions like stress, boredom, or sadness. Find alternative ways to cope with emotions besides eating.

- **Example:** If you're feeling stressed, consider taking a short walk or practicing deep breathing instead of reaching for a snack.

Step 9: Reflect After the Meal

- **Reflection:** After you finish your meal, reflect on how it made you feel. Notice whether you feel satisfied and nourished.

- **Example:** After a homemade soup, reflect on the warmth and comfort it provided, and how it nourished your body.

Step 10: Practice Consistently

- **Consistency:** Make mindful eating a regular practice. The more you engage in mindful eating, the more it becomes a natural part of your daily life.

Mindful eating can lead to a greater appreciation of food, better digestion, and healthier eating habits. By incorporating these steps into your meals, you can savor your food more fully and develop a mindful approach to nourishing your body and enjoying the pleasures of eating.

Enjoying food and life is about more than just the act of eating. It's about savoring the entire dining experience, from the preparation of a meal to the pleasure of sharing it with loved ones. Here's a step-by-step guide on how to fully enjoy food and life with practical examples:

Step 1: Embrace the Cooking Process

- **Cooking as a Journey:** Approach cooking as a creative journey rather than a chore. Embrace the process of selecting ingredients, experimenting with flavors, and preparing meals with joy.

- **Example:** When making homemade pizza, involve your family in choosing toppings and shaping the dough. Enjoy the laughter and messiness of the process.

Step 2: Choose Quality Ingredients

- **Ingredient Selection:** Opt for high-quality ingredients whenever possible. Fresh, seasonal produce and premium cuts of meat can enhance the overall dining experience.

- Example: When making a salad, use locally sourced, organic vegetables and fresh herbs to elevate the flavors.

Step 3: Create a Pleasing Ambiance

- **Ambiance:** Set the mood for a delightful dining experience by creating a pleasing ambiance. Consider lighting, music, and table decor to enhance the atmosphere.

- **Example:** When hosting a romantic dinner, dim the lights, play soft music, and arrange candles on the table for a cozy atmosphere.

Step 4: Share with Loved Ones

- **Shared Meals**: Share meals with family and friends. Dining together fosters connections, strengthens relationships, and creates cherished memories.

- **Example**: Invite friends over for a potluck dinner, where everyone contributes a dish, and enjoy the communal experience of sharing food.

Step 5: Savor Each Bite

- **Mindful Eating**: Practice mindful eating by savoring each bite. Take the time to appreciate the flavors, textures, and aromas of your food.

- **Example**: When indulging in a piece of rich chocolate cake, close your eyes and savor the decadent taste with each forkful.

Step 6: Celebrate Food Traditions

- **Cultural Traditions:** Explore and celebrate different food traditions and cuisines from around the world. Trying new dishes can be an exciting way to enjoy diverse flavors.

- **Example**: Host a themed dinner night dedicated to a specific cuisine, like Mexican tacos, complete with traditional dishes and decorations.

Step 7: Disconnect from Distractions

- **Unplug:** Disconnect from electronic devices and distractions during mealtime. Engage in conversations and be present with your dining companions.

- **Example:** Put away your smartphone and have an uninterrupted conversation over a candlelit dinner.

Step 8: Practice Gratitude

- **Gratitude:** Cultivate a sense of gratitude for the food you have and the ability to enjoy it. Reflect on the abundance in your life.

- **Example**: Before eating, take a moment to express gratitude for the meal, the people you're sharing it with, and the moments you're creating.

Step 9: Explore Culinary Adventures

- Adventure in Cooking: Challenge yourself to explore new cooking techniques, ingredients, and recipes. Embrace culinary adventures to keep your passion for food alive.

   - Example: Try your hand at making sushi rolls from scratch or experiment with a cuisine you've never cooked before.

Step 10: Live in the Moment

   - Living Fully: Finally, embrace the idea that life is meant to be savored. Enjoy food as one of life's pleasures and relish every moment you spend around the table.

   - Example: When dining at a picturesque outdoor café, take in the scenery, savor the delicious meal, and appreciate the present moment.

By following these steps and examples, you can fully enjoy food and life, making each dining experience a celebration of flavors, relationships, and the beauty of the present moment.

CONCLUSION

In the culinary journey we've embarked upon together, we've explored the art and science of cooking like a professional, from selecting the finest ingredients to mastering essential techniques. We've delved into the secrets of crafting natural sauces, elevating plate presentation, and understanding the significance of mindful eating. Our quest has extended beyond the kitchen, touching on the joy of sharing meals, embracing food traditions, and living life to the fullest.

Cooking, at its heart, is not just about nourishing the body but also about nurturing the soul. It's a creative endeavor that allows us to express ourselves, connect with others, and find joy in the simple act of preparing and sharing food. Through the culinary skills and knowledge you've gained, you're now equipped to embark on your culinary adventures with confidence and finesse.

As we conclude this culinary journey, we want to express our heartfelt gratitude for joining us on this exploration of the culinary world. We hope you've found inspiration and valuable insights that will enrich your cooking experiences and, ultimately, your life. May your kitchen be a place of creativity, your table a source of connection, and your meals a celebration of the beauty in every bite.

Thank you for sharing this culinary voyage with us, and we wish you a lifetime filled with delicious dishes, memorable moments, and the sheer joy of enjoying food and life to the fullest.

Bon appétit and happy cooking!